SURPRISING STARTS
HEALTH AND HYGIENE
PRODUCTS

FANTASTIC FAILURES
From Flops to Fortune

MARTIN GITLIN

45 45TH PARALLEL PRESS

Published in the United States of America by Cherry Lake Publishing Group
Ann Arbor, Michigan
www.cherrylakepublishing.com

Reading Adviser: Beth Walker Gambro, MS, Ed., Reading Consultant, Yorkville, IL
Series Adviser: Virginia Loh-Hagan
Book Designer: Frame25 Productions

Photo Credits: © Kallayanee Naloka/Shutterstock, cover, title page; © Mongkolchon Akesin/Shutterstock, 4; © AshTproductions/Shutterstock, 5; © medijucentras/Shutterstock, 7; CardioNetworks: Drj, CC BY-SA 3.0 via Wikimedia Commons, 8; Public domain, United States Patent Office, 9; © Goncharov Igor/Shutterstock, 10; Official photographer, Public domain, via Wikimedia Commons, 13; Ministry of Information Photo Division Photographer, Public domain, via Wikimedia Commons, 14; © Walter Cicchetti/Shutterstock, 15; Britta Gustafson, CC BY-SA 2.0 via Wikimedia Commons, 19; Lambert Pharmacal Company, Public domain, via Wikimedia Commons, 20; Lambert Pharmacal Company, Public domain, via Wikimedia Commons, 21; © kiraziku2u/Shutterstock, 22; Nicola Perscheid, Public domain, via Wikimedia Commons, 25; Wilhelm Röntgen; current version created by Old Moonraker., Public domain, via Wikimedia Commons, 26; © Tridsanu Thopet/Shutterstock, 27; © Mark_Kostich/Shutterstock, 28; © Aleksandr Yu/Shutterstock, 29; © Birgit Reitz-Hofmann/Shutterstock, 32

45th Parallel Press is an imprint of Cherry Lake Publishing Group.

Library of Congress Cataloging-in-Publication Data

Names: Gitlin, Marty, author.
Title: Surprising starts of health and hygiene products / by Martin Gitlin.
Description: Ann Arbor, Michigan : 45th Parallel Press, [2024] | Series: Fantastic failures: from flops to fortune | Audience: Grades 4-6 | Summary: "Failed inventions and unexpected uses abound in this look at the contribution of failures to the health industry. Fantastic Failures: From Flops to Fortune takes readers through the unexpected origins of popular products and innovations. With a focus on persistence and creative thinking, this hi-lo series makes the case that failure might just be the first step to success"-- Provided by publisher.
Identifiers: LCCN 2023043765 | ISBN 9781668938249 (hardcover) | ISBN 9781668939284 (paperback) | ISBN 9781668940624 (ebook) | ISBN 9781668941973 (pdf)
Subjects: LCSH: Medicine--History--Juvenile literature. | Discoveries in science--Juvenile literature. | Hygiene products--History--Juvenile literature. | Health products--History--Juvenile literature.
Classification: LCC R133.5 .G58 2024 | DDC 610/.9--dc23/eng/20230921
LC record available at https://lccn.loc.gov/2023043765

Cherry Lake Publishing would like to acknowledge the work of the Partnership for 21st Century Learning, a network of Battelle for Kids. Please visit Battelle for Kids online for more information.

Printed in the United States of America

Note from publisher: Websites change regularly, and their future contents are outside of our control. Supervise children when conducting any recommended online searches for extended learning opportunities.

Contents

INTRODUCTION

"If at first you don't succeed, try, try again." This is an old saying. It's been said a lot. It's a great tip. Failure is part of life. It's not bad. It can have good results. People must not let failure defeat them. They should keep trying. Failing can lead to success.

Scientists learn from their mistakes. They know about failing. They have ideas. They do tests. But not all ideas work. Some ideas **flop**. *Flop* means to fail. Ideas may not work as planned.

Successful people don't give up. They solve problems. They find other uses for flops. They turn flops into fortunes.

The world of health has many examples. People's health is important. Many great inventions started as failures. These failures worked out. They saved people's lives. They improved their lives.

Successful scientists show **persistence**. Persisting means not quitting. Their hard work paid off. That is a lesson everyone can learn.

CHAPTER 1

Pacemakers: From Listening Device to Pace Setter

. . . .

Failure is only bad when nothing is learned from it. Wilson Greatbatch found that out. Greatbatch was an inventor. He was also an **engineer**. Engineers design and build things. Greatbatch loved testing things. He loved trying things. Sometimes what he tried failed. But he never gave up. That trait led to a life-saving invention.

It all started in 1956. Greatbatch wanted to record human heartbeats. He used a recorder. He added the wrong tool. The machine didn't record heartbeats. Instead, it produced electronic **impulses**. Impulses are forces.

Greatbatch made a mistake. But he still listened closely. He heard pulses. He heard a steady beat. It sounded like a healthy heart. This gave him an idea. Greatbatch came up with a plan. He realized his new device could help sick hearts. It could send shock waves to the heart. That would help heart muscles receive and send blood.

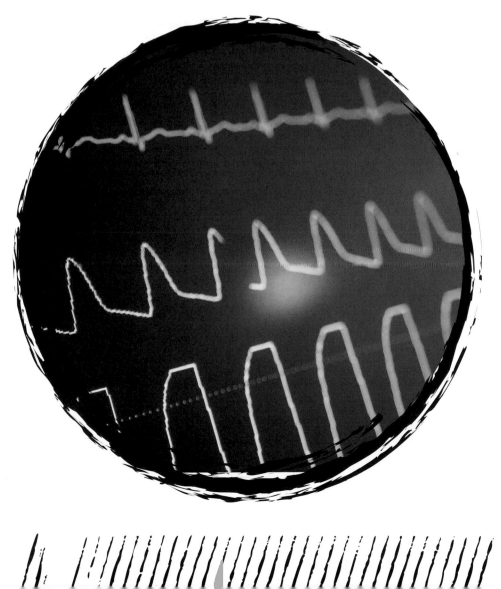

Greatbatch was excited. He walked to his barn. The barn was behind his home. He had a lab there. He continued his work there. He turned his mistake into a useful device. He invented the first **pacemaker**. Pacemakers are planted inside the body. They help maintain a steady heartbeat.

The average human heart beats once a second. When it does not, it can be deadly. People can die from a bad heart. This would be a fast death. Greatbatch knew that. He knew his device was important. The first pacemaker was used in 1960. It was placed inside a human. It began saving lives.

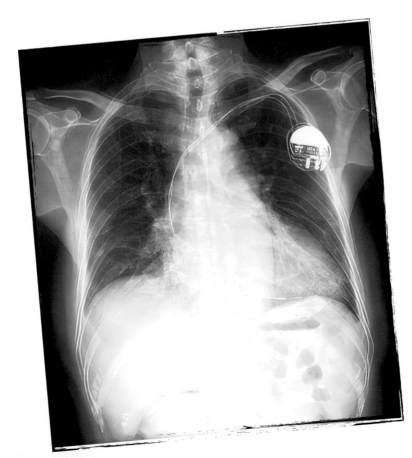

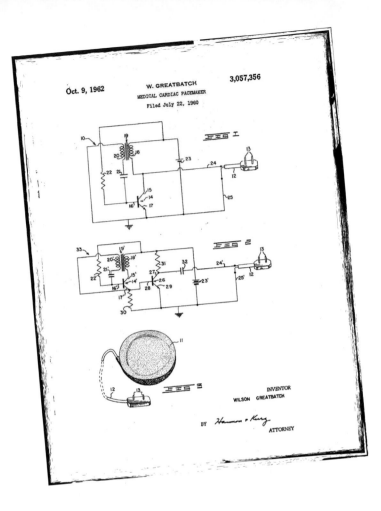

Greatbatch invented many things. He had **patents** on over 325 inventions. Patents are legal rights. They protect inventors. Greatbatch studied cures. He wanted to treat sicknesses. He worked on new kinds of fuel. He wanted to help our planet. He did many good things. But he was most proud of his pacemaker.

He earned many awards. He was invited to be in the National Inventors Hall of Fame. He received a medal from President George H. W. Bush. This happened in 1990.

Greatbatch refused to let failure beat him. He kept asking questions. He found answers. His pacemaker has kept millions of people alive.

FLOPPED!

Elixir Sulfanilamide, the Killer Medicine

Antibiotics are special drugs. They kill **bacteria**. Bacteria are cells. Elixir Sulfanilamide was invented in 1937. It was an antibiotic. It was meant to kill bacteria. Instead, it killed people. It was not a cure. It was a poison. It was made by the S. E. Massengill Company. This company was a drug company. It didn't do enough testing. The drug was sold too early. The result was a disaster. More than 100 users died. Some used it to get rid of simple problems. For example, some people took it to cure sore throats. They ended up dead. From this tragedy came one positive outcome. The public demanded more testing of drugs. This helped shape the Food and Drug Administration (FDA).

CHAPTER 2

Penicillin: Discovery in a Dirty Dish

....

Alexander Fleming was a British scientist. He took a vacation in 1928. This vacation changed the world.

Fleming returned to his lab. He had forgotten to clean it. He came home to dirty **petri dishes**. Petri dishes are small dishes. They're clear. They're used to grow cells. Fleming's dishes contained **mold**. Mold is the growth of fungus. It's found on damp or decaying matter.

Most people would throw away moldy things. Or they'd clean them out. Fleming saw something interesting.

He studied the mold. He noticed how it affected cells. The mold stopped cells from growing. It made a chemical. This chemical killed cells. Fleming gave the mold a name. He called it **penicillin**.

He wanted the world to know. He wrote about his findings. He spoke about it. He shared it with the medical field. He was shocked by their responses. People showed little interest.

Fleming kept going. He knew penicillin was helpful. Several **chemists** worked with him. Chemists are scientists. They tried to make pure penicillin. But they failed. One said the task was impossible.

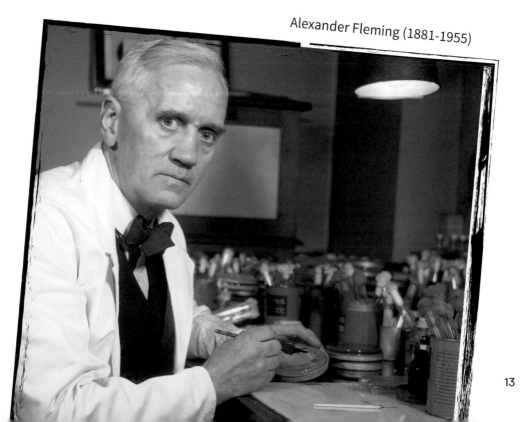

Alexander Fleming (1881-1955)

Fleming couldn't figure out the problem in his lifetime. But his idea survived. A team of scientists became interested. They launched the Penicillin Project in 1937. They did tests. They debated. They kept failing. Their product couldn't safely be used as medicine. But they kept trying.

They finally found success. They tested the drug on mice in 1940. They infected 8 mice with disease. Four mice received penicillin. They were the only mice to live. This was great news! Penicillin worked.

But one big problem remained. Gallons of mold produced little penicillin. The mold took up a lot of space. The team used bathtubs to store it. They needed a way to make lots of penicillin. They couldn't make enough. There was a shortage. A police officer got a cut. He got an infection. He used penicillin. But his supply ran out. He died 5 days later.

Then World War II (1939–1945) began. British scientists couldn't focus on penicillin anymore. The scientists worked on the war effort instead.

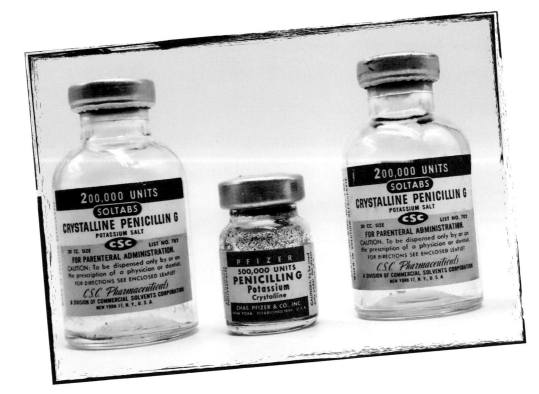

The Penicillin Project shifted to the United States. Scientists in Illinois got busy. Lots of corn is grown there. Corn is treated. This process breaks down corn kernels. Special corn water is made. This water was waste. But scientists found a use for it. They mixed it with the mold. This produced lots of penicillin.

Better ways to increase production were found. Mary Hunt was a lab assistant. She discovered another way. She went to a store. She saw a rotting melon. The melon had mold. Melon mold made even more penicillin.

Soon American drug companies got involved. The United Stated entered World War II in 1941. Many soldiers were sick and hurt. These soldiers needed penicillin. Scientists kept working.

Two years later, there was plenty of penicillin. It was made widely available. People around the world used it. Penicillin is a wonder drug. It's among the most important drugs ever created. And it all started with Fleming going on vacation without cleaning his dishes.

FLOPPED!
Misguided Medicine: Bloodletting

Medicine has come a long way. But scientists and doctors were sometimes wrong. Long ago, they thought bad blood made people sick. They tried to remove the bad blood. They practiced bloodletting. Doctors cut patients. They cut into an elbow or knee. They let the blood drain. The patient got dizzy. The patient passed out. Usually, about 20 ounces (591.5 milliliters) of blood was drained. Then the doctors covered the cut. The patient's body made more blood. Doctors thought the new blood would be good blood. It would cure the patient. But there was never any bad blood. Bloodletting never helped cure anyone. It may have even led to the deaths of George Washington and Mozart.

CHAPTER 3

LISTERINE®: A Mouthwash that Cleaned Floors

LISTERINE® is a mouthwash. It's well-known. It's one of the oldest products. It's named after Joseph Lister. Lister was an English doctor. He believed in keeping operating rooms free of germs. He helped create **antiseptic** medicine. Antiseptics fight infections. They stop the growth of bad germs.

Lister did not invent LISTERINE®. But he inspired it. He used antiseptics. He used them for surgeries. He put them on the skin. This stopped infections.

Joseph Lawrence invented LISTERINE® in 1879. This happened in St. Louis, Missouri. Lawrence was a doctor. He created a special antiseptic. His product was made for surgical purposes. He named it in honor of Lister. He worked with Jordan Wheat Lambert. Lambert owned a drug company. He helped sell LISTERINE®.

People soon found other uses for it. They used it to get rid of **dandruff**. Dandruff is dry skin on scalps. People rubbed it on their armpits. They did this to reduce odors. People also used it as a floor cleaner. But it was mostly used as a mouthwash. It was marketed to dentists. People swished it in their mouths. They did this for better breath.

LISTERINE® was first sold by **prescription**. Prescriptions are written orders from doctors. By 1914, prescriptions were no longer needed. LISTERINE® was available to all. It was the first mouthwash sold in stores.

Gerald Barnes Lambert was Jordan's son. He became the company's president. Lambert was a great salesman. He knew how to promote LISTERINE®. He created ads. He turned bad breath into a social problem. He presented LISTERINE® as the solution.

His ads showed young men and women turned off by bad breath. People hated the idea of having bad breath. They wanted to avoid it. They thought it would hurt their social lives. They didn't want to be around others with bad breath. So they bought LISTERINE®.

Germs in the mouth cause **plaque**. Plaque is the buildup of food bits. It hardens. It's tough to remove. Brushing teeth alone doesn't remove plaque. Plaque can cause bad breath. It also makes teeth look ugly. People started to care about dental health. This increased sales as well.

Lambert convinced people they needed Listerine. People thought it removed plaque and germs. LISTERINE®'s slogan is well-known. It is "Kills germs that cause bad breath." Sales soared. Most products from the 1870s are long gone. But LISTERINE® is still popular. It's used every day.

FLOPPED!
The Fen-Phen Weight Loss Drug

Millions of people try to lose weight every year. They want to be healthier. They want to be thinner. Many companies try to sell diet pills. Diet pills are a big business. But drugs that promise weight loss often fail. And some can be dangerous. Some can be deadly. One such drug was Fen-Phen. It was introduced in the 1990s. Some doctors told patients to try it. They thought it was safe. Fen-Phen was prescribed to 18 million people. People wanted to shed pounds. Fen-Phen worked. But it had one big problem. It caused damage to the heart. It was taken off the market in 1997.

CHAPTER 4

Mysterious Glowing Gas Leads to X-ray Technology

It was December 22, 1895. Wilhelm Röntgen was a German **physicist**. Physicists are scientists. They study matter and energy. Röntgen was in his lab. He was working with special glass tubes. The tubes produced beams. The beams showed images on a screen.

Röntgen noticed something odd. He filled the tube with a special gas. He sent an electric charge through it. There was a strange glow. It showed through the tube. Röntgen didn't know what it was.

The glow passed through paper. It passed through wood. It even passed through skin. It cast shadows of solid objects onto film.

Röntgen named his discovery "X-ray." That is because he didn't understand what it was. He didn't know what else to call it. X is used to describe things unknown.

Wilhelm Röntgen (1845-1923)

Röntgen invited his wife into the lab. Her name was Anna Bertha Röntgen. She became the first human to be x-rayed. Röntgen x-rayed her hand.

That glow became known as **radiation**. Radiation is a type of energy. It moves outward from something. It moves in waves.

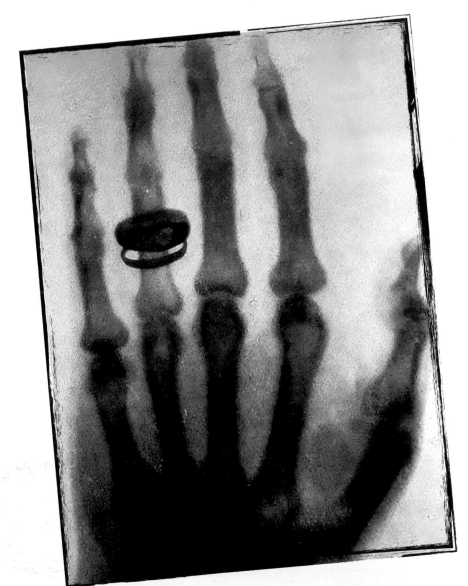

Interest in x-rays grew. X-ray machines were invented. Doctors used them. They could see inside human bodies. They could see bones. They could see organs like lungs. They could see damage inside the body. X-rays helped doctors figure out what's wrong. They were first used on a patient on January 11, 1896. A doctor x-rayed his friend. He saw a metal needle. The needle was stuck inside his hand. X-rays are common practice now.

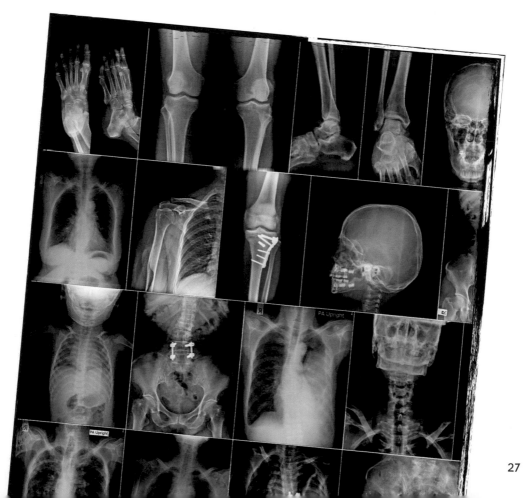

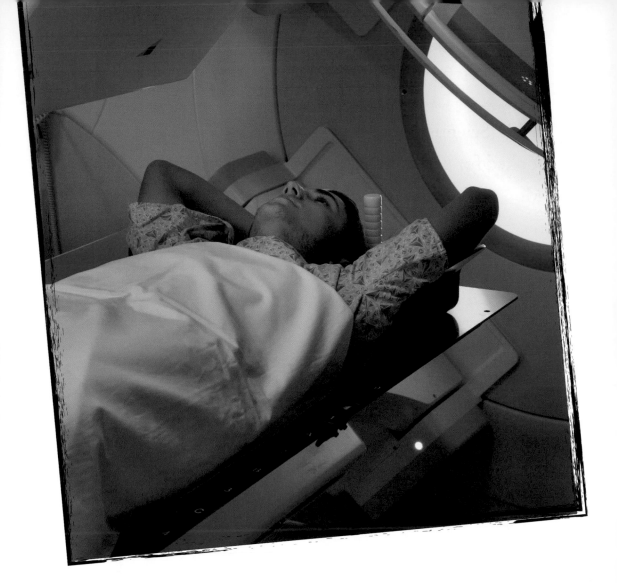

The science of radiology was born. Scientists
studied more ways to use x-rays. Soon patients were
being treated through radiation. X-rays are aimed at
diseased cells. They're used to kill deadly cancer cells.
But it isn't all good. Radiation can be dangerous. Too
much radiation is harmful. It's poisonous.

X-rays gained greater use in the 1950s. That is when more was learned. X-rays were also used in other fields. Scientists scanned blades on a jet plane. They looked for cracks. A crack could destroy a jet plane. More uses were found. X-rays are used at airports. They scan luggage. Dangerous items can be found and removed. X-rays save lives.

Smartphones and computers also use x-ray beams. This makes x-rays a part of our daily lives.

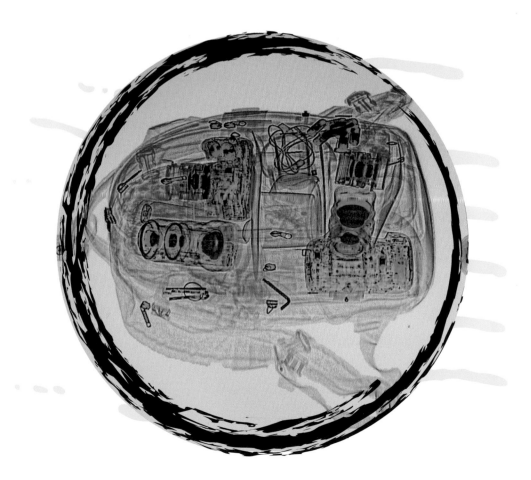

BEHIND THE SCENES
Radiation and Hair Loss

Too much radiation can cause hair loss. William Dudley was a chemistry professor. He worked at Vanderbilt University. He studied the effects of radiation. He tested it on himself. He x-rayed his own head. His hair fell out in one spot. He was the first to publish about it. He did this in 1896. A child had been shot. Doctors wanted to find the bullet. The child was sent to Vanderbilt. The child's head was x-rayed for an hour. This was a long time. Soon the child lost hair. A bald spot formed on his head. He wasn't the only one. Others lost hair as well. They had all been affected by too much radiation. This discovery was later used in a useful way. X-rays were used to remove unwanted hair. This became popular in salons.

LEARN MORE

Books

Jones, Charlotte Foltz. *Mistakes That Worked: The World's Familiar Inventions and How They Came to Be.* New York: Delacorte Press, 2016.

Loh-Hagan, Virginia. *Medicine.* Ann Arbor, MI: Cherry Lake Publishing, 2022.

Loh-Hagan, Virginia. *Strange Medicine.* Ann Arbor, MI: Cherry Lake Publishing, 2018.

Mould, Steve. *The Bacteria Book: The Big World of Really Tiny Microbes.* New York: DK Children, 2018.

Wagner, Kristie. *Human Anatomy for Kids: A Junior Scientist's Guide to How We Move, Breathe, and Grow.* Berkeley, CA: Rockridge Press, 2021.

Websites

With an adult, explore more online with these suggested searches.

"History of Medicine/Kids Work!" Know It All

Kids Health

"X-rays," Britannica Kids

GLOSSARY

antibiotics (an-tee-bye-AH-tiks) drugs used to stop or kill bacteria

antiseptic (an-tuh-SEP-tik) a substance that fights infection

bacteria (bak-TEER-ee-uh) one-celled organisms that live in soil, water, plants, or animals

chemists (KEM-ists) scientists who study chemicals and their properties

dandruff (DAN-druhf) a common scalp condition in which small pieces of dry skin flake off the scalp

engineer (en-juh-NEER) a designer and builder of engines or other complex structures

flop (FLAHP) to fail

impulses (IM-puhls-uhs) forces that moves in waves

mold (MOHLD) the growth of a fungus, usually on damp or decaying matter

pacemaker (PAYS-may-ker) an artificial device for stimulating the heart muscle and regulating its contractions

patents (PA-tuhnts) government documents allowing someone the sole right to make and sell an invention

penicillin (peh-nuh-SIH-luhn) an antibiotic used to treat many types of infections

(continued on next page)

GLOSSARY (continued)

persistence (per-SIH-stuhns) the will to keep trying after first failing or experiencing challenges

petri dishes (PEE-tree DISH-uhz) shallow, clear dishes used for growing cells

physicist (FIH-zuh-sist) a scientist who studies matter and forces in the universe

plaque (PLAK) food particle buildup in the mouth

prescription (prih-SKRIP-shuhn) a written order by a doctor to a patient for medicine

radiation (ray-dee-AY-shuhn) energy that moves outward in the form of waves or particles

INDEX

ABOUT THE AUTHOR

Martin Gitlin is an educational book author based in Connecticut. He won more than 45 awards as a newspaper sportswriter from 1991 to 2002. Included was a first-place award from the Associated Press for his coverage of the 1995 World Series. He has had more than 200 books published since 2006. Most of them were written for students.